Need to Know

Multiple Sclerosis

Alexander Burnfield

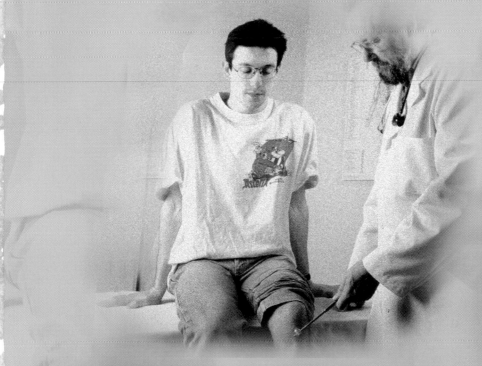

Heinemann
LIBRARY

www.heinemann.co.uk/library

Visit our website to find out more information about **Heinemann Library** books.

To order:

 Phone 44 (0) 1865 888066

 Send a fax to 44 (0) 1865 314091

 Visit the Heinemann Bookshop at www.heinemann.co.uk/library to browse our catalogue and order online.

Produced by Monkey Puzzle Media Ltd
Gissing's Farm, Fressingfield, Suffolk IP21 5SH, UK

First published in Great Britain by Heinemann Library, Halley Court, Jordan Hill, Oxford OX2 8EJ, part of Harcourt Education.
Heinemann is a registered trademark of Harcourt Education Ltd.

Editorial: Katie Orchard
Design: Jane Hawkins
Picture Research: Sally Cole
Production: Viv Hichens

Originated by Ambassador Litho Ltd
Printed and bound in Hong Kong, China by
 South China Printing Company

ISBN 0 431 09764 X
08 07 06 05 04
10 9 8 7 6 5 4 3 2 1

The author wishes to thank his wife, Penny, for her help in preparing the manuscript and his niece, Catherine Reynell, for reading it through. He is also grateful to the Multiple Sclerosis Trust and Multiple Sclerosis International Federation for their help, and to Ernest Hecht for his support.

British Library Cataloguing in Publication Data
Burnfield, Alexander
  Multiple Sclerosis. – (Need to know)
  1.Multiple sclerosis – Juvenile literature
  I.Title
  616.8'34

Acknowledgements
The publishers would like to thank the following for permission to reproduce photographs:
Alamy pp. 33 (Myrleen Cate/Photo Network), 41 (ImageState); Corbis pp. 10 (Hulton-Deutsch Collection), 20 (Paul Barton); Getty Images pp. 5 (Stone), 16 (Image Bank), 17 (Image Bank), 19 (Image Bank), 36–37 (Image Bank); Terence Keane p. 37 (National Multiple Sclerosis Society); Mary Evans Picture Library p. 8–9 (Sigmund Freud Copyrights); MS Trust pp. 27, 42; Photofusion p. 13 (Crispin Hughes); Rex Features p. 43 (Helen Osler); Science Photo Library pp. 1 (CC Studio), 4 (Custom Medical Stock Photo), 6 (Jon Meyer/Custom Medical Stock Photo), 7 (Athenais, ISM), 14 (CC Studio), 15 (Geoff Tompkinson), 23 (Scott Camazine), 24, 25 (Dr. John Zajicek), 31 (BSIP Laurent), 32 (Claire Paxton and Jacqui Farrow), 34 (James King-Holmes), 39 (Peter Menzel), 47 (Philippe Plailly), 48 (James King-Holmes), 49; Topham Picturepoint/ImageWorks pp. 28, 29, 44–45, 50–51.

Cover photographs reproduced courtesy of Science Photo Library/Dr John Zajicek and Photofusion/Crispin Hughes.

Contents

Any words appearing in the text in bold, **like this**,
are explained in the Glossary.

Multiple sclerosis

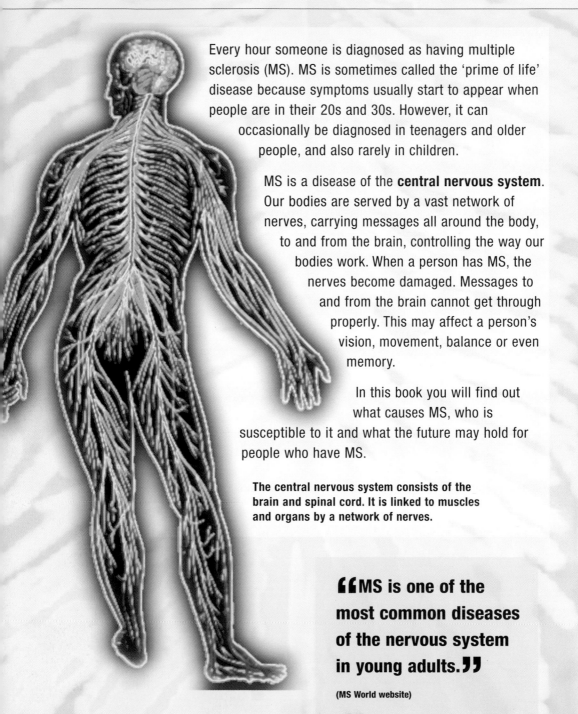

Every hour someone is diagnosed as having multiple sclerosis (MS). MS is sometimes called the 'prime of life' disease because symptoms usually start to appear when people are in their 20s and 30s. However, it can occasionally be diagnosed in teenagers and older people, and also rarely in children.

MS is a disease of the **central nervous system**. Our bodies are served by a vast network of nerves, carrying messages all around the body, to and from the brain, controlling the way our bodies work. When a person has MS, the nerves become damaged. Messages to and from the brain cannot get through properly. This may affect a person's vision, movement, balance or even memory.

In this book you will find out what causes MS, who is susceptible to it and what the future may hold for people who have MS.

The central nervous system consists of the brain and spinal cord. It is linked to muscles and organs by a network of nerves.

❝MS is one of the most common diseases of the nervous system in young adults.❞

(MS World website)

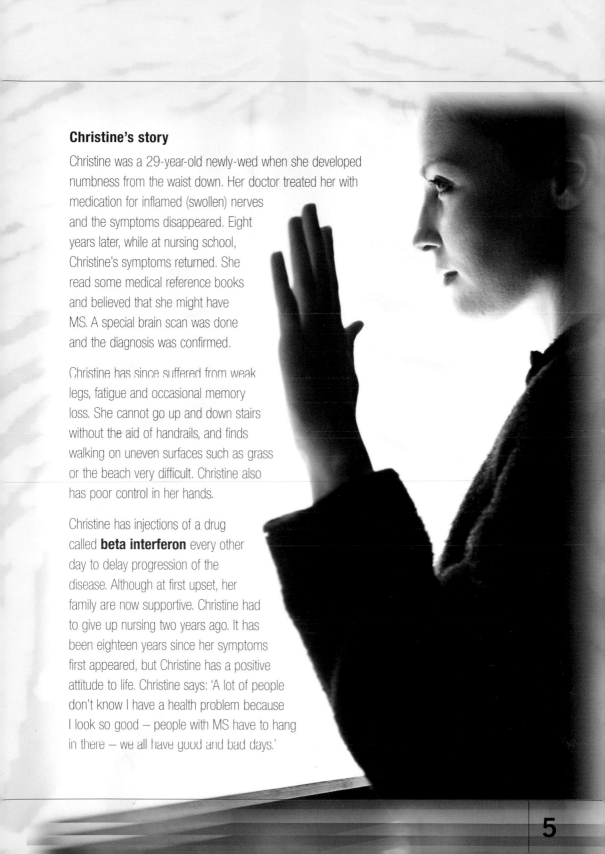

Christine's story

Christine was a 29-year-old newly-wed when she developed numbness from the waist down. Her doctor treated her with medication for inflamed (swollen) nerves and the symptoms disappeared. Eight years later, while at nursing school, Christine's symptoms returned. She read some medical reference books and believed that she might have MS. A special brain scan was done and the diagnosis was confirmed.

Christine has since suffered from weak legs, fatigue and occasional memory loss. She cannot go up and down stairs without the aid of handrails, and finds walking on uneven surfaces such as grass or the beach very difficult. Christine also has poor control in her hands.

Christine has injections of a drug called **beta interferon** every other day to delay progression of the disease. Although at first upset, her family are now supportive. Christine had to give up nursing two years ago. It has been eighteen years since her symptoms first appeared, but Christine has a positive attitude to life. Christine says: 'A lot of people don't know I have a health problem because I look so good — people with MS have to hang in there — we all have good and bad days.'

What is MS?

About one in 1,000 people in populations of European origin have MS. In Australia for example, it is estimated that there are 20,000 people who have the disease. Every day in Canada, three people are diagnosed with MS.

A disease of the central nervous system

MS is a disease that targets the **central nervous system** – the brain and the spinal cord. The brain is the control centre for the whole body. Messages from the brain travel down the spinal cord to the muscles in the body and limbs. Messages also travel back to the brain up the spinal cord from the skin and joints. These messages are sent along the nerves as electrical impulses. Some tell muscles to move, and control how they work together. Other nerves from the skin and joints alert the brain to sensations such as vibration, temperature, pain and the body's position.

A healthy spinal cord. It consists of nerves that conduct messages to and from the brain.

Nerves are protected by a fatty, insulating substance called **myelin**. In people with MS the myelin is damaged in places. The electrical impulses are blocked in different parts of the brain, spinal cord and nerves.

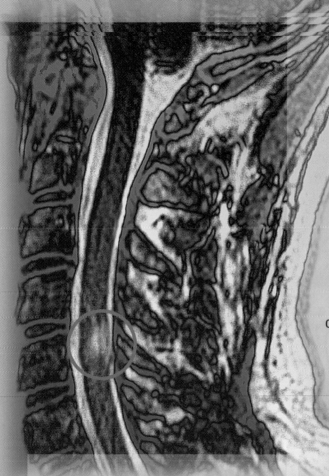

come and go and are not the same for everyone with the disease. In a mild case a person might just have periods of intense tiredness (fatigue); in severe cases they may be paralyzed.

Nerve cells under attack

The word **sclerosis** means scarring. The disease looks like 'many scars' to someone looking at the brain or spinal cord tissue of a person with MS. Some damage that occurs in MS is thought to be caused by an abnormal response to infections. The **immune system** (the body's natural defence system) produces **white blood cells** that destroy harmful bacteria or viruses. Many scientists believe that when some people with MS develop infections the white blood cells function abnormally, attacking healthy tissue such as myelin and nerve cells. The destruction of healthy tissue by the immune system is called an **auto-immune response**.

A spinal cord damaged by MS. A lesion (scar) is circled in pink, just to the right of the spine.

This stops nerves carrying their signals effectively. This is what causes the early symptoms of MS – weakness, numbness, loss of balance or loss of vision, for example. But, unlike many other diseases, the symptoms that occur in MS are unpredictable – they

History of MS

Throughout history, there have probably always been people who suffered from MS. However, it was not until the 1860s that the symptoms were linked to a specific disease. Before MS was recognized as a disorder of the **central nervous system**, people were sometimes referred to as having the 'creeping paralysis', because symptoms mysteriously crept up on a person over a period of time.

Early cases

One of the earliest recorded cases of possible MS was a woman who became known as the Virgin Lidwina of Schiedam, Holland (1380–1433). She was the daughter of a labourer and one of nine children. Details of her illness came from her biographer, the Franciscan priest, Johannes Brugman (1400–1473), who acquired information from relatives, her priest and confessor, and local clerics. Lidwina developed a series of MS-like symptoms following a fall while ice-skating when she was sixteen. For the rest of her life she experienced unpleasant pains, and difficulties with walking and using her arms. She developed blindness and had problems swallowing. During her life she

believed that her illness was sent by God and that she was a victim for the sins of others. She also had some strange **hallucinations**. After her death a chapel was built on her grave. She was eventually made a saint for her suffering and patience, and is regarded as the patron saint of ice-skaters!

Another early case of MS, of which there is now no doubt about the diagnosis, is that of Sir Augustus D'Este (1794–1848). He was the grandson of King George III of England and a cousin of Queen Victoria. It is said that he was the first person ever to be diagnosed as having MS after he had died. He suffered initially from blurred vision and then developed fatigue (excessive tiredness, often associated with MS), heat intolerance, **spasms** and difficulty walking. Eventually he used a wheelchair to get around. He died 26 years after his first symptoms appeared. His diary, which describes his experiences of the disorder, is now in the collection of the Royal College of Physicians, London.

In 1868 a French scientist, Jean-Martin Charcot, first recognized and defined MS. Sometimes referred to as the 'Father of MS', Charcot was one of the founders of the science of **neurology** (the study of disorders of the nervous system). He demonstrated that there was a link between patients' symptoms, and areas of **inflammation** and scarring in certain parts of the brain and spinal cord.

Jean-Martin Charcot (fourth figure from the right) teaching at the University Hospital in Paris.

New discoveries

While Jean-Martin Charcot was the first to recognize MS as a disease, he never understood what caused it or how it might be treated. During the 20th century many more discoveries were made. Each new discovery is like a piece of

Lord Edgar D. Adrian (right) won the Nobel Prize for Medicine in 1932.

a jigsaw puzzle – as the pieces are put together the picture of MS gradually becomes clearer.

In 1916 Dr James Dawson of Edinburgh University in Scotland examined the brains of people who had died of MS, using a newly discovered way of showing up nerve cells under a microscope. A fatty substance surrounding nerves, **myelin**, had first been discovered in 1878 by the French anatomist, Louis-Antoine Ranvier, but Dawson was now able to see this in detail. He noted that in the brains of the MS sufferers, there was inflammation around the blood vessels and damage to the myelin around some nerves. This is a key feature of MS.

In 1925, British researcher Lord Edgar Douglas Adrian discovered that nerves carry electrical impulses (which we now know carry messages from the brain to different parts of the body and back again).

Working with others, he showed that these impulses were impaired when the surrounding myelin became damaged. Lord Adrian, together with Sir Charles Scott Sherrington, won the Nobel Prize for their discoveries of how nerve cells work.

Research on animals

In 1935 Dr Thomas Rivers at the Rockefeller Institute in New York found a way of creating an MS-like disease in laboratory animals. This laboratory model of MS was used to provide clues as to how MS worked. It led to the discovery that the body's natural defence system against disease (the **immune system**) could go wrong and attack its own tissue – the myelin.

Jigsaw puzzle

The discoveries in the early 20th century have been the foundation all of modern research. More and more pieces of the MS jigsaw puzzle have been put in place, but research into the disease has not yet been completed. When the last piece of the puzzle is laid, it will not be so much a breakthrough as the end result of hard and painstaking work carried out by scientists around the world for more than 100 years.

Types of MS

MS does not affect everyone in the same way. Symptoms may vary in severity, and not everyone will end up needing to use a wheelchair. There are four main types of MS: benign; relapsing/remitting (RRMS); secondary progressive (SPMS); and primary progressive.

Benign MS

Benign MS is the mildest form of MS. About 10–20 per cent of sufferers have benign MS. They may experience occasional attacks (which are called **relapses**) with periods of complete recovery (which are called **remissions**) in between. People with benign MS become only mildly disabled, and many have no disability at all. They have evidence of some MS damage on medical examination or brain scans but may experience very few symptoms. This is because the damage is either minimal, or in places in the brain or spinal cord that do not cause obvious disability.

Relapsing/remitting MS (RRMS)

More than half of people with MS begin with **relapsing/remitting MS**. They have relapses, about two or three times per year or sometimes less frequently, with a partial or complete remission in between. But as time goes on, usually after several years, symptoms may worsen because of the gradual death of the nerve cells themselves, in addition to damage to the **myelin** sheaths surrounding them. At this stage the type of MS changes to SPMS.

Secondary progressive MS (SPMS)

Most people with RRMS (above) eventually develop **secondary progressive MS**. After a few years, the frequency of relapses and remissions usually lessens, but the extent of disability increases due to the loss of the nerve cells. A person with MS can be said to have SPMS when they no longer have relapses and remissions but experience progressive disability instead. So this type of MS is called 'secondary' because the disability has become progressive after several years of a relapsing and remitting stage.

Primary progressive MS

About 10 per cent of people with MS become increasingly disabled over a period of several years without having any remissions. They gradually become more and more disabled without experiencing sudden worsening or periods of improvement in their symptoms. This type of MS is called **'primary' progressive MS** because progression is from the first symptom onwards with no relapsing/remitting phase.

This woman has quite severe MS. Most people with the disease show fewer signs of disability.

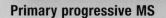

Diagnosis and investigations

There is at present no definitive test for MS – the doctor must make a decision based on several factors and rule out other possible conditions. In this way the doctor builds up a picture of the disease until a diagnosis is possible.

Clues in a patient's medical history

If a patient has typical symptoms and signs of MS occurring in different parts of the brain and spinal cord at different times, a diagnosis of MS can sometimes be made from the patient's medical history. For example a person may have experienced a period of blurred vision aged 20, and two years later have a weak left leg together with some pins and needles in their right hand. This initial diagnosis will be followed up by a **neurological** examination. The doctor will test the patient's strength, vision, co-ordination, reflexes and ability to feel different types of sensation. He or she looks for evidence of neurological damage, such as an extra jerky response to a tap under the knee or changes in the appearance of the optic nerve seen at the back of the eye through a special illuminated lens.

Checking a person's knee-jerk reflexes can reveal damage in the spinal cord.

❝A disease does not exist until it has a name.❞

(Charles Rosenberg, Professor of the History of Science at Harvard University, USA)

Investigations

The body's natural response to infection is to produce lots of **white blood cells**, which fight disease (see page 7). In people with MS, the protective **myelin** covering nerve fibres also comes under attack from the white blood cells. One important laboratory test is the examination of the fluid that surrounds the brain and spinal cord (called **cerebrospinal fluid**). The fluid is extracted through a hollow needle that is inserted into the patient's spine in a procedure called a **lumbar puncture**. If the tests show an increase in white blood cells or a particular change in the chemical make-up of the cerebrospinal fluid, this can indicate that the patient has MS.

Another test for MS involves looking at the electrical activity in the nerves connected with the patient's vision, hearing or sensation. If there is a delay in electrical impulses travelling through a nerve, compared with what is usual in a healthy nerve, this may indicate that the patient has MS.

Doctors also use a special brain scan – a **magnetic resonance image (MRI) scan** to look for the hidden signs of MS. The MRI scanner uses a harmless magnetic field and radio waves to produce a detailed image of the brain and spinal cord. It can show up damaged areas of myelin, called **lesions**.

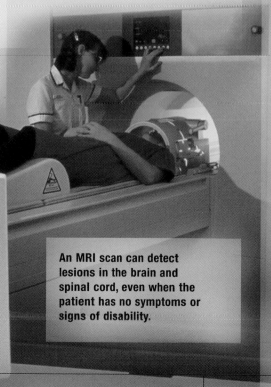

An MRI scan can detect lesions in the brain and spinal cord, even when the patient has no symptoms or signs of disability.

Symptoms of MS

Our spinal cords contain millions of nerves, all carrying messages from the brain to different parts of the body and back again. Each nerve cell is protected by a **myelin** sheath. When a person has MS, the nerves' myelin becomes damaged, blocking the messages to and from the brain.

Depending on where in the body the nerve damage occurs, this may produce a range of symptoms.

Vision

Damage to one or both of the **optic nerves** (the nerves carrying messages from the eye to the brain and back again), may result in blurred vision. People with MS frequently suffer from eye problems, but rarely lose their sight completely. Normal vision usually returns in four to twelve weeks, but some people with MS are left with

Blurred vision coming on suddenly in one eye is a common symptom of MS.

blind spots or more serious visual loss. Another common eye symptom is seeing double. This can occur early on in MS and people may remember having had this problem for many years before they developed other signs of the disease.

Sensation and pain

Another common symptom for people with MS is clumsiness of one arm. This is due to nerve damage in the spinal cord blocking the messages to and from the joints, fingers and skin. Pins and needles, or numbness in the hands and feet, can be early symptoms of MS. Some people have burning or other types of pain in their legs, arms or the trunk of their bodies. A few people experience a shooting, stabbing pain in the face, like a toothache. This form of **neuralgia** (nerve pain) affects the nerve carrying sensations from the face area. Other types of pain can occur in MS, often due to damaged nerves in a particular area of the body.

People with MS can find it difficult to pick things up because of impaired co-ordination.

Movement and balance

MS sufferers may also experience contraction and stiffness of muscles, affecting the arms, legs and trunk of the body. This may result in painful muscle **spasms**. Most commonly this can affect the legs. In severe cases there is complete paralysis of a person's legs and they are unable to walk. Nerve damage in one part of the brain can cause balance problems and **tremor** (uncontrollable shaking). People who have difficulty with their balance still have some strength in their arms and legs, but they cannot control them properly. This makes it difficult for them to handle objects or walk easily.

The MS bladder

Another common problem that MS sufferers experience is difficulty with bladder control. Several different nerves connect to the muscles of the bladder and to the ring of muscle at its neck, which allows us to control it. Nerve damage of the spinal cord can therefore lead to complicated **urinary** symptoms. The most common include passing urine frequently and having to go urgently. **Incontinence** can also be a problem – this is when people cannot hold on to their urine and wet themselves. Our kidneys act as a natural filter system, taking away impurities and waste products, passing them through the bladder and out of our bodies as urine. People with MS who have bladder control problems are more likely to get bladder or kidney infections due to stagnant urine in the bladder – so they must drink plenty of fluids.

Other symptoms

Some men and women with MS may experience difficulties in sexual relationships but they can have babies. The problems are caused by the nerves in the sexual organs, which do not function properly. Sometimes people with MS develop slurred speech and other communication problems. Some people may also find it difficult to swallow, and become at risk from chest infections if food goes down the wrong way and reaches the lungs. In people who are paralyzed by MS, and those who spend a lot of time in a wheelchair or in bed, there is a risk that **pressure sores** will develop. This is because the skin is deprived of

MS symptoms file

A person with MS may have three or four of the following symptoms, but not usually all at once:

- blurred or double vision
- loss of vision in one eye
- severe fatigue
- weakness of limbs, especially legs
- poor co-ordination and balance
- tremors
- dragging feet
- numbness and 'pins and needles'
- burning sensations
- loss of bladder control
- difficulties with memory
- slurred speech.

For people with MS, exercise, heat, infections and large meals can cause severe fatigue.

blood and oxygen if a person stays in one position for too long. But pressure sores do not occur when there is good nursing care.

Fatigue and memory

As well as physical symptoms, MS can lead to memory difficulties, confusion or emotional problems in some people. It also produces an overwhelming feeling of tiredness called MS fatigue. (This is explained more fully on pages 38–39.)

Who gets MS?

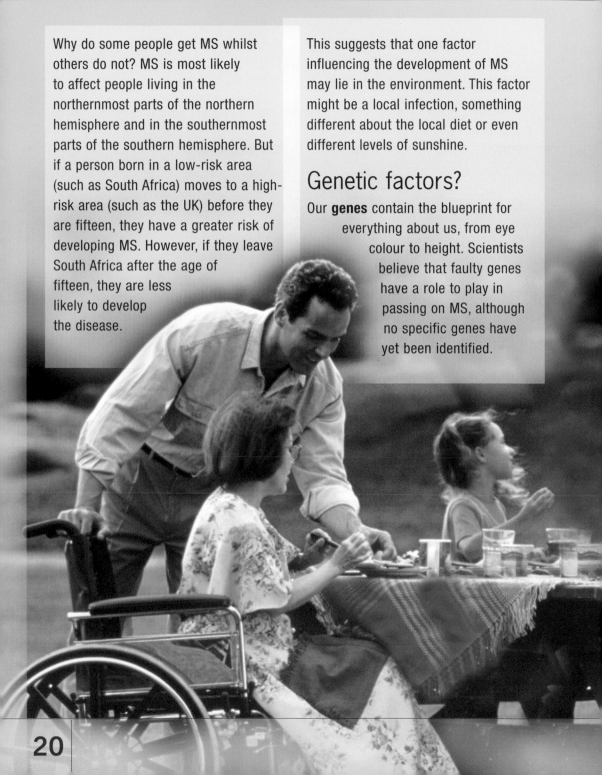

Why do some people get MS whilst others do not? MS is most likely to affect people living in the northernmost parts of the northern hemisphere and in the southernmost parts of the southern hemisphere. But if a person born in a low-risk area (such as South Africa) moves to a high-risk area (such as the UK) before they are fifteen, they have a greater risk of developing MS. However, if they leave South Africa after the age of fifteen, they are less likely to develop the disease.

This suggests that one factor influencing the development of MS may lie in the environment. This factor might be a local infection, something different about the local diet or even different levels of sunshine.

Genetic factors?

Our **genes** contain the blueprint for everything about us, from eye colour to height. Scientists believe that faulty genes have a role to play in passing on MS, although no specific genes have yet been identified.

Scientists do not yet understand why, but women are more likely to develop MS than men – in the USA the ratio is about two women to one man. While MS is not believed to be **hereditary** (directly passed on from a parent to a child), it does seem to run in families, which suggests that a **susceptibility** (tendency) to the disease can be inherited. MS is quite common in Scandinavia, but the 'Lapp' people who live there develop it infrequently. They are of Asiatic origin and have a different genetic make-up from the fair-skinned peoples of the same region. We know that Northern European populations are at greater risk of MS than African or Asian people. Similarly, no pure-blooded Aboriginal Australian, different in racial origin from those of European origin, has ever been diagnosed with MS.

When a person has MS, the whole family has to adjust and cope with the disease.

Did the Vikings spread MS?

One theory suggests that MS may have been carried and spread by the Vikings. The Vikings terrorized Northern Europe around 1000 CE. Later their descendants, including the Normans, invaded and occupied many parts of the world. Wherever they went they mixed with the local population and left many offspring to pass on their genes. Today MS is most common in countries settled by people of Northern European origin. While there is no conclusive genetic proof, the evidence is strong enough to point an accusing finger at those marauding sea-farers.

How does it develop?

When a person has MS, they develop lesions (areas of damage) in particular parts of the brain and spinal cord. These lesions are preceded by **inflammation** and an increase in **white blood cells** around certain nerve cells. The protective **myelin** sheath, which surrounds the nerve cell like a layer of insulation, is lost as result of this process. When the myelin is damaged or lost, the electrical impulses (messages to and from the brain) travelling up or down the nerve are slowed down or stopped. Later, as the course of the disease develops, the nerve cells themselves may die. This is the reason why **relapsing/remitting MS** often develops into **secondary progressive MS** (see page 12).

Nerve messages delayed or stopped

When there is nerve-cell damage or loss, messages do not reach the brain from sensory areas in the skin, eyes, or joints. Other messages going from the brain to groups of muscles are also

" One morning, about eight years ago, I awoke to find I could not see through my right eye. It was as though a film of cloud was covering it. I lay still for a while with my eyes closed, hoping that when I opened them all would be clear. Again, I opened my right eye, but with the same result. "

(John Mythen, Canadian cartoonist and author of the cartoon book *Claude MSing Around*)

Tom's story

Tom is aged 49. He has **primary progressive MS** (see page 13). Tom has experienced gradually increasing weakness in both legs over the last seven years. He also has difficulties controlling his bladder. He has never had a **remission** and his condition has become progressively worse. Stiffness in his muscles is controlled by medication, but Tom now has to use a wheelchair to get around. He continues to work at a specially adapted office as a computer technician.

delayed or stopped. This interference in the way nerves carry messages is responsible for the symptoms of MS (see pages 16–19). When such damage occurs in the brain or spinal cord, symptoms do not always develop.

Sometimes messages can find new pathways around the damage using other nerve cells. However, a few small **lesions** situated in important areas of the brain or spinal cord can cause more severe disability.

This brain scan clearly shows MS lesions on the brain as yellow patches.

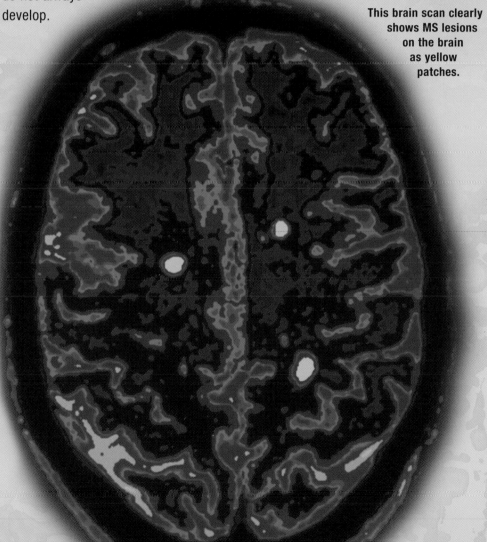

The mystery of what starts MS

The exact cause of MS remains a mystery. One theory suggests that MS might be the delayed affect of a virus acquired in childhood but causing damage years later. Another possibility is that the disease is started by an infection completely unlike a normal virus or bacterium. Such infections have been shown to cause other diseases of the **central nervous system**, such as **Creutzfeld-Jacob disease (CJD)**.

Researchers have claimed that specific viruses have been identified in the microscopic examination of tissues from some people with MS. One virus under suspicion is **Human Herpes Virus 6 (HHV-6)**. The **Epstein Barr Virus (EBV)** may also be involved in causing MS. This virus is better known for causing glandular fever – a common throat infection in young people, which leads to swollen and painful glands and a sore throat, and causes general weakness and tiredness. At the moment, however, there is no scientific proof that any particular virus plays a part in MS, and people with MS may have been infected by a combination of viruses.

Myelin sheaths (the fatty substance around nerves) enable electrical impulses to travel along the nerves quickly, taking messages to and from the brain.

The body's defences go wrong

MS sufferers may have a genetic defect in their **immune system**, but scientists are not yet sure how this affects them. If a person's immune system is not functioning properly, it might allow a virus to remain in the body for longer than normal, or an attempt to rid the body of a virus might damage the body's own tissue. This is called an **auto-immune response**. It seems likely that an auto-immune response to an infection plays a part in the development of MS, as it does in the cases of other diseases such as diabetes.

In response to an infection, the immune system produces more white blood cells to fight against it. But if a person's immune system is not functioning properly, the white blood cells may also attack healthy tissue. In the case of MS it is the myelin surrounding nerve cells that is damaged. We know that MS **relapses** commonly occur after a viral infection such as a cold or the 'flu. This could mean that MS is made worse by all infections when they stimulate the body's immune system, further encouraging the production of destructive white blood cells.

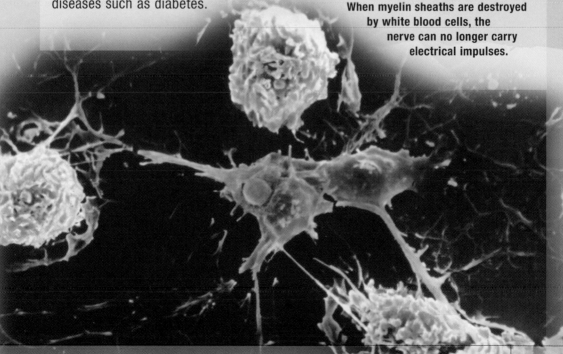

When myelin sheaths are destroyed by white blood cells, the nerve can no longer carry electrical impulses.

Managing MS

A person diagnosed with MS will see a wide range of professional people. Doctors and MS nurses all help with the treatment and management of the disease. They work with other health and social workers when necessary. They also put MS sufferers in contact with local MS groups and the MS Society.

Doctors

The diagnosis of MS is made by a doctor who specializes in **neurology** (treatment of diseases of the **central nervous system**). He or she listens to the patient's symptoms, carries out a physical examination and performs tests (see pages 14–15). It can take a long time to complete all the tests and this may be a period of anxiety and confusion for the patient and their family. The doctor keeps the patient informed of progress and confirms the diagnosis only when there is enough evidence.

Some people with MS can be shocked, disbelieving, frightened or angry when the condition is first diagnosed. They may feel that they have not been told quickly enough or they may even think that the neurologist has made a mistake. People can ask for another opinion about diagnosis or treatment if they want to. A good doctor will work in close partnership with his or her patient and appreciate their fears and frustrations, taking the time to listen to the patient's questions about their condition. It is important that the person with MS is given information about the disease together with

emotional support. The family doctor or GP will usually be the key person managing the treatment of MS after the diagnosis has been made. He or she will arrange whatever support and back-up is needed.

Nurses and counsellors

Sometimes a counsellor will be able to help a person or family come to terms with MS and make adjustments in their lives. Counsellors provide help and support. They are professionals in their own right but much counselling is also done by the various health and social care professionals – in particular by the MS nurse who is trained in dealing with all aspects of the disease. Many people in families with MS find they have the resources to help each other without needing to involve counsellors, but there should be regular contact with a trusted doctor to ensure the best possible long-term care is obtained.

Continuing to work

When a person has MS they usually hope to carry on working so they can bring money into the family and continue to make a contribution to their community. Work is also important for a person's self-respect. MS has an impact on how well someone can work and if they are disabled, it can also make getting to work, climbing stairs and even using the toilet more difficult. People with MS are often affected by increasing tiredness, or fatigue – this can lead to loss of concentration and affect a person's ability to do some types of work. People with MS can continue working when their difficulties are understood. A person's working space and their method of working can be adapted to suit their particular disability.

Professor Barbara Jordan, a former US congresswoman and businesswoman who had MS, continued to live a full and active life for many years.

Advice and therapy

An **occupational therapist** is a professional who can advise a person and their employer how to make helpful changes after they have assessed their abilities and needs. Simple changes can often make it possible for people with MS to continue working.

For example a person can be given a work space nearer to the toilet or provided with a desk where there is room for a wheelchair. Flexible working hours and a place for rest may also help.

A wheelchair-adapted car can give a person with MS greater independence.

Making it easier

People who have MS will often need help with getting around. Cars can be specially adapted with hand controls instead of foot pedals, or people can be helped to use taxis or adapted public transport. Provisions can be made for wheelchairs, and elevators can be provided. Many countries have laws ensuring that there is no discrimination against disabled people accessing and using the workplace, but good employers and colleagues will want to help anyway. Many people with MS are able to continue working as long as there is goodwill and understanding, and changes are made – but others may not be able to work as before. They can be helped to find fulfilment in other ways, such as voluntary work, and may benefit from financial support from the government.

Managing MS

It is important for people with MS to look after themselves properly. This includes following a healthy diet, avoiding situations that make the condition worse, and sticking to advice given by healthcare professionals.

Keeping fit and healthy

There is no specific diet that has been proved to affect the course of MS, but there is some evidence from research that people with the disease should minimize their intake of animal fats, and increase the amount of **polyunsaturated fats** and fish oils. But it is most important to eat a well-balanced diet with plenty of fruit, vegetables and fibre. Being overweight, smoking and drinking alcohol to excess can worsen MS symptoms.

Staying cool

Many people with MS function best in cool but not cold surroundings. They must avoid hot places, too many bedclothes and hot baths, which all make symptoms worse. Vacations can create anxiety for people with MS. Help will need to be organized in advance at airports and railway stations.

If the holiday destination is hot then the person with MS will need reliable air conditioning and access to proper healthcare facilities.

Complementary therapies

Complementary therapies are not cures for MS but they can improve a person's sense of well-being, give enjoyment, and relieve depression and feelings of isolation.

- Aromatherapy is a gentle form of massage using aromatic oils. It promotes relaxation and can help relieve stress.

- Reflexology involves massaging the feet in a special way. This is believed by some to improve a person's health and well-being.

- Music, art or dance therapy helps increase a person's confidence, feelings of well-being and self-respect.

- Massage involves squeezing and smoothing muscles in the client's body – particularly in the neck, back, arms and legs. This helps to relax muscles, reduce **spasms** and increase mobility.

- Yoga enables someone to maximize the strength they have, to learn relaxation skills, and to improve general posture through stretching and meditation.

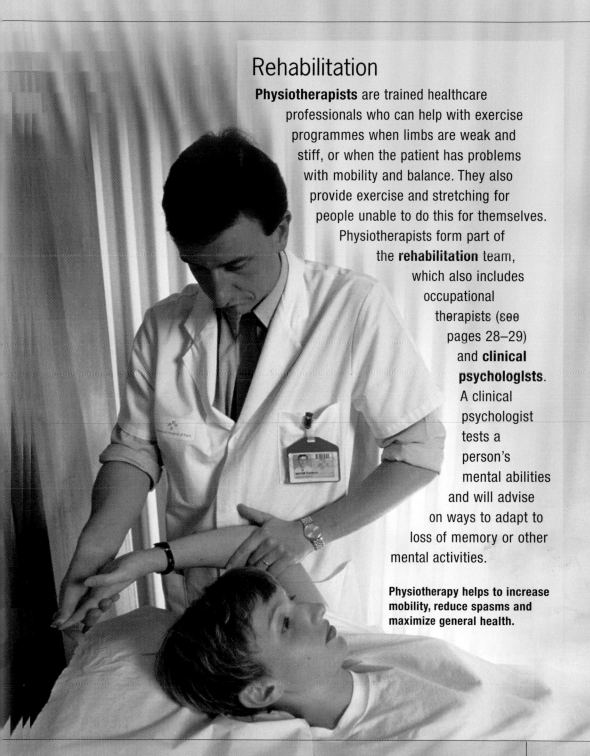

Rehabilitation

Physiotherapists are trained healthcare professionals who can help with exercise programmes when limbs are weak and stiff, or when the patient has problems with mobility and balance. They also provide exercise and stretching for people unable to do this for themselves. Physiotherapists form part of the **rehabilitation** team, which also includes occupational therapists (see pages 28–29) and **clinical psychologists**. A clinical psychologist tests a person's mental abilities and will advise on ways to adapt to loss of memory or other mental activities.

Physiotherapy helps to increase mobility, reduce spasms and maximize general health.

Treating MS

In the early stages of MS people are often prescribed medication called **corticosteroids**. These can sometimes reduce the severity or length of a **relapse**. They work by reducing **inflammation** in nerve tissue and can be taken as tablets or injected directly into a vein. They are only given for short periods of time because prolonged use causes side effects, such as high blood pressure or weakened bones. Other medications are available to relax muscles and reduce muscle stiffening and **spasms**. Some can weaken the muscles too much, so a doctor has to judge the dose carefully to get the right balance for the patient. There are also some medications that help reduce MS fatigue.

Nerve stimulation

Functional electrical stimulation (FES) can also help some people with weak muscles. A small box sends electrical stimulation to paralyzed muscles so that the person can regain useful movement. This is connected to a pressure pad in a shoe that enables the impulse to be triggered when walking, improving mobility.

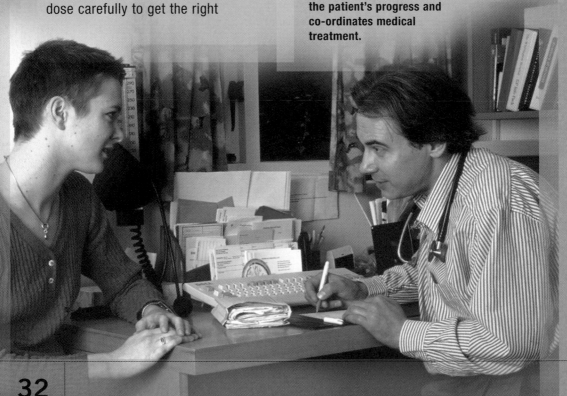

The family doctor monitors the patient's progress and co-ordinates medical treatment.

Regaining bladder control

Difficulties with bladder control in MS can be a major problem. People feel embarrassed about **incontinence** and worry about leaving their homes to work or socialize. This can make them feel very isolated, a disability in itself. But there is help available. Medications can be taken to relax the bladder muscles. Absorbent pads can be used if the problem continues. There are also various urine-collecting devices available, which connect to bags that are worn under a person's clothes. But if medication alone does not work there is an effective way of regaining continence. The person with MS can be trained to insert a sterile **catheter** – a thin, slippery plastic tube – into their bladder. This is called **intermittent self-cathcterization (ISC)**. The tube is inserted through the penis in men and urethral opening in women. This is done every four or five hours, completely emptying the bladder.

Good personal hygiene is essential to avoid the risk of infections.

"With proper symptom management, people rarely need to be treated for MS in hospital."

(The Multiple Sclerosis Trust, 2002)

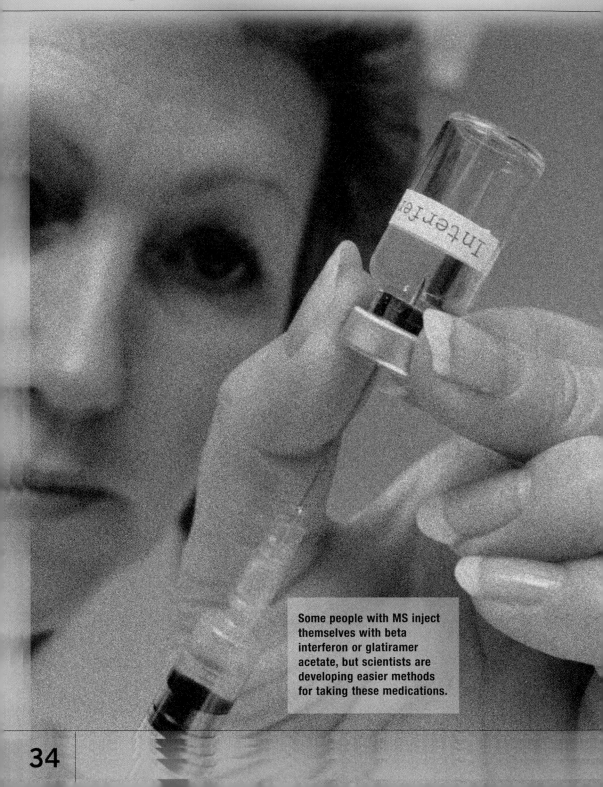

Some people with MS inject themselves with beta interferon or glatiramer acetate, but scientists are developing easier methods for taking these medications.

New medicines for MS

There is no cure for MS, but there are some new medications available that slow down the disease when relapses are frequent and especially disabling. **Beta interferon** is a genetically engineered copy of a protein that occurs naturally in the body. It is given by injection and works by regulating the **immune system** and by fighting viral infections. Research has shown that taking beta interferon can reduce the severity and frequency of relapses by 30 per cent. This greatly increases the quality of a person's life. However, beta interferon does not reverse damage, and has not been proved to prevent permanent disability.

An alternative to beta interferon is **glatiramer acetate**. This works by preventing **myelin** damage and it must be injected once a day. Another disease-modifying medication is **Novantrone**. This suppresses the immune system. However, it can cause serious side effects so Novantrone is only given in severe cases. It is administered directly into a vein every three months.

False treatments

Unfortunately, there are many claims by ignorant or unscrupulous people of other treatments and cures. People with MS and family members wish to believe that they will work, and will often spend lots of money on these 'quack' treatments for which there is no scientific proof. They may become disappointed or angry when they do not work – or they may believe that they really do work and try to convince others. Examples of these misleading claims include removing all the mercury fillings from teeth, or sitting in a special oxygen chamber for hours at a time.

Many people with MS have **remissions** that occur naturally for no obvious reason. They may think they have 'discovered a cure' if they are trying out a new 'treatment' at the time of a natural remission. Quacks are quick to take advantage of this!

Living with MS

People vary in the way they cope with MS. Some people become quite disabled but appear to cope well and live a positive and rewarding life. Others with less disability may experience unhappiness and a feeling that life has become meaningless.

Coming to terms with MS

How a person copes often depends on how well they have adjusted to past problems and what sort of personality they have. For example a perfectionist may find it harder to accept change than a person who has a happy-go-lucky approach to life.

The way a person deals with MS might also depend on how much help they get from their family and friends. Someone living alone with little family contact may cope well if they have understanding and supportive friends. But a person living at home may feel trapped and frustrated if family members try to protect them too much and do everything for them.

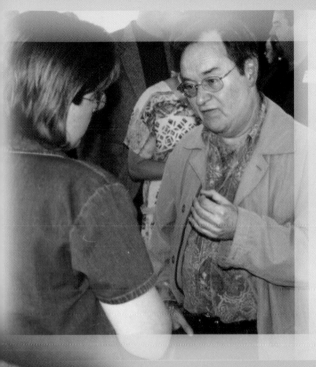

"I know, at first, when I was diagnosed with it I couldn't say 'multiple sclerosis'. Not because I have MS but just the thought of admitting to this disease, it sounded so powerful just saying the words that I just couldn't get myself to say it at first... I kept my MS a secret for fifteen years."

(David 'Squiggy' Lander, Hollywood actor, pictured left)

Many MS sufferers find the constant uncertainty about when the next **relapse** will strike very stressful. It takes time for a person to come to terms with MS and adjust to a new image of themselves. Many are shocked when they first find out they have MS – they can find it hard to believe and accept, and get angry with those around them. But more often they go through a period of sadness and loss until they come to accept MS as something they can live with. They need to keep a balance between giving in to MS and trying to pretend it is not there. But with understanding and support, a person who has MS will often be able to come to terms with it.

MS fatigue

Everyone feels tired some of the time, but for people with MS the sensation of fatigue is more extreme. It is a special kind of tiredness due to muscle weakness and the impaired functioning of the brain, spinal cord and nerves. This is one of the symptoms that people with MS find most distressing and disabling.

The heat effect

MS fatigue can develop quickly when a person exercises or gets hot, for example when they travel to a hot country or get an infection. People vary in how much fatigue they have and not everyone with MS is exhausted in the same way or by the same conditions. When someone is affected they may feel very tired. They usually experience some worsening of symptoms and have difficulty concentrating. Someone with MS may get into a bath-tub full of hot water feeling fine – but after a few minutes they may begin to feel tired and weak. When they try to get out of the tub they may struggle and need help due to weakness in the legs and difficulty with balancing. In addition they may find their vision is blurred and they have a 'pins and needles' feeling in their hands. Although it does not take long for the fatigue to start, it can take a long time for it to go – they have to cool down first. People with MS are most likely to feel fatigued in the afternoon, when the body's natural temperature cycle is at its highest, and also after big meals.

Larry

Larry is 60 years old. He has a mild form of MS known as **benign MS** (see page 12). His main problem is MS fatigue. He always looks perfectly normal and no one could ever guess that he has had MS for 25 years. His vision is occasionally blurred, especially after a hot bath or in a summer heat wave, but otherwise he feels fit and enjoys going for long walks with his family and dogs.

This patient is being monitored as he exercises in cool water. This is part of a scientific research programme to monitor the effect of heat on MS fatigue.

Misunderstanding fatigue

Because fatigue is invisible to other people, they may not be very sympathetic. Friends sometimes remark how well a person with MS looks, and suggest that they are exaggerating their symptoms. People with MS are occasionally told that they are seeking attention or making it up. Words like these can undermine the trust in relationships with family, friends and professionals.

Other problems

Depression

Having MS can make people feel anxious and stressed, especially at the beginning when there is much uncertainty about what is going to happen to them. People with MS can go through periods of sadness and hopelessness. When these feelings are deep and last for more than two weeks they may have **clinical depression**. A person with depression will often find it difficult to sleep or enjoy food. They lose their zest for life and may not have enough energy to cope with normal family life or work.

Memory loss and emotions

Some people with MS experience problems with their memory and concentration. These symptoms can be worrying, both for the person with the disease and for his or her family – especially if people do not understand that MS is the cause of the difficulties. These symptoms are produced when MS **lesions** affect the area at the front of the brain, which deals with thinking, emotions and problem solving.

Some people with MS may lose control over their emotions – they may cry or laugh for no reason and they may become frightened of over-reacting in front of others. This is embarrassing and can lead to withdrawal from society. These symptoms, like the physical ones, come and go and are made worse by tiredness, infection or stress.

Personality change

A few people with MS become disabled intellectually and are unable to cope with even simple tasks. This is rare, and usually occurs in people who are also severely disabled by physical problems. A few people with MS have a lesser degree of intellectual impairment – people may not understand why they appear self-centred and uncaring of other people's

needs. These symptoms occur when someone with MS loses their ability to put themselves in 'another person's shoes'. Rarely, MS can produce serious **psychiatric** conditions such as **bipolar disorder,** a form of depression in which a person alternates between being deeply depressed and very excited.

MS and the family

When one person in a family has MS then, in a way, the whole of the family has it. Each family member will be affected in different ways. They may feel sad, angry, frightened or confused. It may also be necessary for people to change to new roles in the family – a parent may have to give up work or may not be able to care for their children as before. Teenagers may have to take on extra responsibilities, such as doing the shopping or pushing a wheelchair. Some families break up under the strain, but many others find strengths they never knew they had. One of the main stresses for an MS family is the uncertain nature of the disease – **relapses** occur out of the blue, and it is sometimes difficult to plan ahead. Social engagements, journeys and holidays can be particularly difficult to organize.

Dads with MS may not be able to play football, but they can still share special times with their kids.

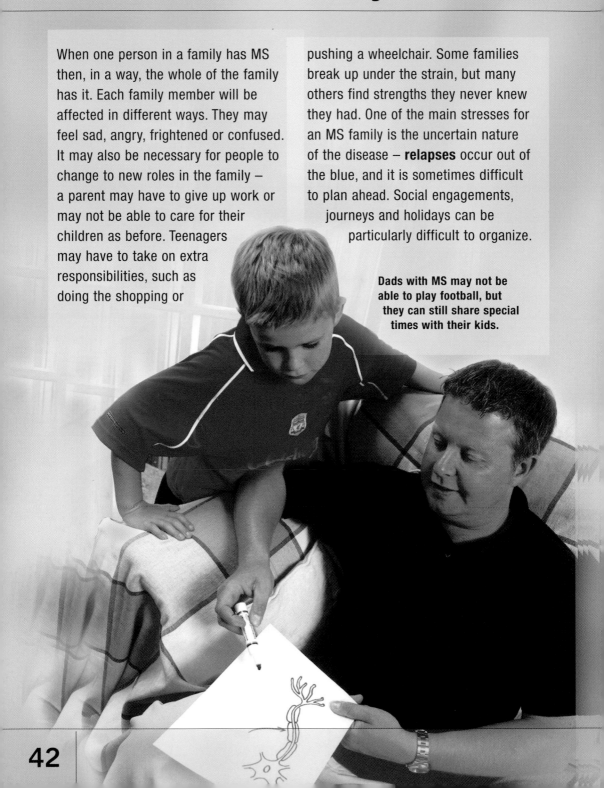

The children of parents with MS can be particularly affected. They may feel ignored and want more attention at home or at school. Some feel confused about what has happened to their parent. They may worry that they will catch MS themselves, or that it is somehow their fault that their parent has MS. Children sometimes feel unreasonably guilty if their mother's illness developed after their birth. Teenagers may find themselves taking on the job of caring for a parent. This can be tiring and lonely work, and it can be difficult for them to go out or have friends round to their home.

Pregnancy

When a woman with MS becomes pregnant she may feel well during pregnancy, but she is more likely to have a relapse after the birth. However, having a baby does not make a woman's MS worse in the long term, although it may be difficult for her to find the energy and strength to look after her children. Most MS families find their own ways of coping, and children of MS families usually mature into especially understanding and practical people.

"They came home and told my sister and me. Di and I went into the kitchen, cried, and swore that we were going to behave like angels from then on – a resolution I think we broke within 48 hours."

(J.K. Rowling, author of the famous Harry Potter books, describing her feelings on learning her mother had MS. She is pictured here, in her role as patron of the MS Society, 2001)

MS and society

Society sometimes treats disabled people as second-class citizens. In the past disabled people were kept out of sight, or even feared. Even today people with disabilities are sometimes avoided, talked down to, ignored or expected to accept second-best. Such negative attitudes towards disabled people can make it more difficult for people with MS to adjust to a new role in life or to ask for help. But when a community welcomes disabled people and understands their problems, people with MS can 'come out' and feel they belong. Of course people with MS are all different individuals with their own strengths and weaknesses, but society can help them to take a full part in everyday life, which in turn can help them to accept their own destiny.

Some MS groups hold sponsored walks, or other activities, to have fun and raise money for research. This walk took place in 1999 in Community Park, Jacksonville, Illinois, USA.

The price of independence

MS costs everyone money because of the extra need for medical and social care, and government funds. But if people are helped to be independent and continue working, they can make their own contribution to the community. They feel better, they contribute more and it costs the community less. Help with transport and easy access to buildings can make an enormous difference. More seriously disabled people may need

special adaptations to their home, such as a ramp for getting a wheelchair in and out, and this can help them to continue living on their own. Some people even have specially trained assistance dogs to help with day-to-day tasks.

Self help

There are many groups that help people with MS to help themselves and each other. In many countries such as the USA, the UK, Ireland, Australia and New Zealand, MS charities give information, support, social contacts and wide-ranging advice. These groups also provide opportunities for self-help and they campaign for special causes – like funding for new treatments or fairer laws for disabled people. The Internet provides even more ways in which a person can source information, look up medical research and make contact with others. Even people who are mostly housebound can make friends and contacts in MS chat rooms, and feel that they are playing a valuable part in the world community of people who have MS.

Will a cure be found?

Research into MS is carried out world-wide and funded either by governments, **pharmaceutical** (medical drugs) companies or MS charities. The National MS Society of the USA has supported research since 1946 and now spends about US$320 million a year on carefully selected research programmes. There are four main areas of study – immunology, genetics, virology and the biology of myelin.

Immunology

Immunology research is now concentrating on finding out exactly what the specific immune responses are that lead to MS. In the future this is likely to lead to safer, more effective medications, with fewer side effects.

Genes

No specific **gene** has been found to cause MS. It is thought that MS is likely to be the result of many genes affecting different aspects of the disease process. Researchers are now comparing the genetic make-up of individuals, twins and ethnically different populations. In this way it is hoped to find out the difference in the genetic make-up of various people who are more or less likely to develop the disease. One day this might mean that gene abnormalities can be prevented or corrected by gene therapy – this means actually changing the genes a person has or modifying how they work. Research is still in the very early stages at the moment.

Viruses and the immune system

Experts in **virology** and bacteriology now believe that the **immune system** in people with MS may deal abnormally with many different types of infection. Learning how the immune systems of individual people deal with infections may lead to further understanding of what goes wrong, and how to prevent an inappropriate **auto-immune response** so that **white blood cells** do not attack healthy myelin (see pages 6–7).

Nerves and myelin

Myelin research is being carried out to find out what factors play a part in nerve damage, how to stop this process and how to repair the myelin. Scientists are even looking at ways to make nerve cells grow again.

"The search for a cure must continue. Sometimes answers come unexpectedly from seemingly unrelated fields within basic biomedical research: more often the route is slow and arduous."

(Sylvia Lawry, founder of the National Multiple Sclerosis Society, USA, and the Multiple Sclerosis International Federation)

Immunologists are working on research into MS.

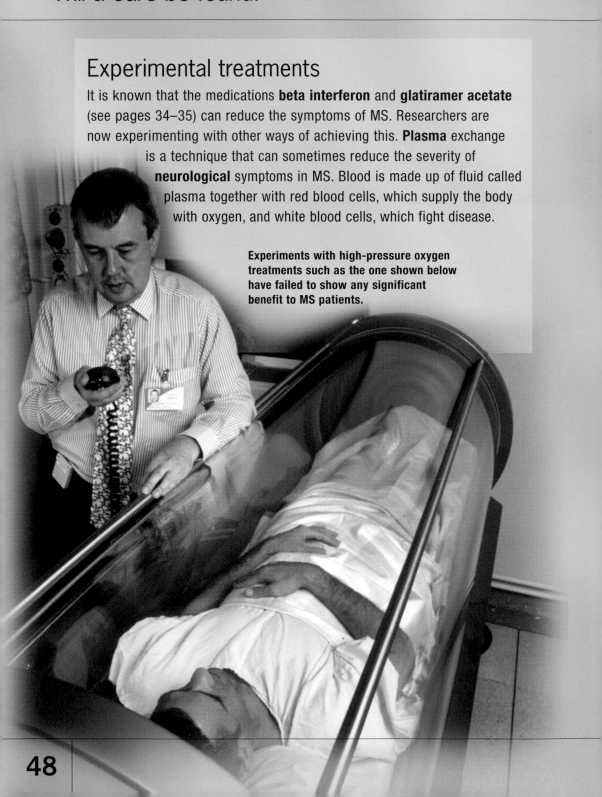

Experimental treatments

It is known that the medications **beta interferon** and **glatiramer acetate** (see pages 34–35) can reduce the symptoms of MS. Researchers are now experimenting with other ways of achieving this. **Plasma** exchange is a technique that can sometimes reduce the severity of **neurological** symptoms in MS. Blood is made up of fluid called plasma together with red blood cells, which supply the body with oxygen, and white blood cells, which fight disease.

Experiments with high-pressure oxygen treatments such as the one shown below have failed to show any significant benefit to MS patients.

Plasma from a person with MS may contain poisonous substances that make MS worse. The plasma exchange procedure separates the patient's blood cells from their plasma. The cells are then mixed with plasma obtained from donors (healthy people without a disease) and the new mixture is put back into the bloodstream. Antiviral medications are also being tried, and may have a part to play in reducing the symptoms of fatigue.

People often feel better if they are given any sort of treatment, even one that has been shown to have no effect on a disease. Research into any new treatment takes this into consideration. To test the reliability of a new drug, it must be compared with a **placebo** – a substance that looks exactly the same, but is known to be ineffective. During the drug trials, the placebo and the medicine to be tested are labelled in code. Neither the people receiving the substances nor the doctors giving them know which is the real drug. At the end of a trial, which may take several years, the researchers unlock the codes and can see if there is a genuine effect. All new treatments for MS are tested in this way to make sure that they are both safe and effective.

Cannabis – the debate

One controversial study is looking into the effectiveness of cannabis (pictured below) in the treatment of MS. Cannabis has been used medicinally for over 2000 years but is now a banned drug in most countries. However, some people with MS claim that cannabis helps reduce their symptoms, especially muscle **spasms**. In 1998 the House of Lords, in the UK, looked at the issue of the medicinal use of cannabis and recommended further studies. Since that time research trials have been set up to find out if these claims are true.

Will a cure be found?

The future is bright

A diagnosis of MS may mean disability, but for most people it is not a death sentence and many will never need a wheelchair. In the last 20 years scientists have learned a great deal about who gets MS, how the disease affects people and what the possible causes might be. MS is not yet curable but there are treatments available that can lessen or eliminate some of the symptoms.

There are also many ways to improve general health and mobility to make it possible for people with MS to live almost normal lives. Sadly, some people with MS do have the disease more severely but society is gradually finding better ways to help, physically, emotionally and financially.

Research into the disease continues, often supported by the voluntary MS organizations. While we do not yet have all the answers, the pieces of the jigsaw puzzle are coming together. We can see how genetic and environmental factors (see page 20) might combine to produce MS – the genes perhaps causing an abnormal response to infection and instead of just fighting the infection also causing damage to the **central nervous system**. It is a bit like an army fighting an enemy, but getting the wrong instructions and attacking its own side. The soldiers have not been given the right orders by their officers and discipline has been lost!

This ten-year-old boy (right) has MS, but it is rare for the disease to affect children.

In the future there is good reason to think that we will find ways of treating MS more effectively or even preventing the disease before it can do any damage. Information about MS is now readily available to everyone. It is important that people with MS fully understand the disease. Knowing the facts about MS empowers people to come to terms with the illness and seek out effective and scientifically proven ways to fight this destructive and disabling condition.

❝Even with my physical limitations, I know that there is so much I can do.❞

(Karen Model, who has MS, attending the Jimmy Heuga Can-Do Center, USA)

Information and advice

Most countries have an MS Society or similar voluntary organization, and there is also an international federation that supports and helps to develop these charities. MS Societies usually have local groups that provide direct help for people in the community. Many offer online discussion groups for people with MS and their relatives, including children and teenagers. There are also some good booklets and newsletters available to young people. It is worth checking with the charities directly to obtain the most up-to-date information on research, publications and various support groups.

Contacts in the UK

MS Society of Great Britain and Northern Ireland
372 Edgware Road, London NW6 6ND
Tel: +44 (0) 20 8438 0700
Website: www.mssociety.org.uk/
The MS Society is the UK's largest charity for people affected by Multiple Sclerosis – about 85,000 people in the UK.

Multiple Sclerosis Trust
Spirella Building, Bridge Road, Letchworth, Hertfordshire SG6 4ET
Tel: +44 (0) 1462 476700
Fax: +44 (0) 1462 476710
Website: www.mstrust.org.uk/
The Multiple Sclerosis Trust is a leading independent UK charity for people with MS, and offers a high standard of education to nurses and other healthcare professionals.

Jooly's Joint
Website: www.mswebpals.org/
Jooly's Joint is a friendly, informative and positive site for people with MS, and their families. It also has a number of lists including ones for carers and younger people.

Contacts in the USA

The National Multiple Sclerosis Society of the United States of America
733 Third Avenue, New York, NY 10017, USA
Tel: (1) 212 986 3240
Toll Free Number: 1 800 344 4867
Website: www.nationalmssociety.org/
The mission of the National Multiple Sclerosis Society is to end the devastating effects of MS.

Keep S'Myelin
Website: www.nationalmssociety.org/keepsmyelin/index.html
This is a website for children of people who have MS.

The Multiple Sclerosis Foundation
Website: www.msfacts.org
The MSF's primary mission is to ensure the best quality of life for those coping with MS by providing comprehensive support and educational programmes.

MS World
Website: www.msworld.org/
The MS World worldwide Internet 'family' includes thousands of people from around the world diagnosed with MS.

Contacts in Australia

National Multiple Sclerosis Society of Australia
Suite 503, Level 5, 157 Walker Street,
North Sydney, NSW 2060, Australia
Tel: (02) 9955 0700
Website: www.mssociety.com.au/
MS Australia strives for a world without MS through quality research, and for service excellence to people with MS and their carers. They run children's and family camps and provide one-to-one information.

Contacts in New Zealand

Multiple Sclerosis Society of New Zealand
4th Floor, Hallenstein House, 276–278
Lambton Quay, PO Box 2627, Wellington,
New Zealand
Tel: 0 4 499 4677 or 0800 2 435767
MS NZ exists to promote a united voice, and an environment in which members can work together to encourage research development for the benefit of all people with MS.

International contacts

Multiple Sclerosis International Federation
3rd Floor, Skyline House, 200 Union Street,
London SE1 0LX Tel: +44 (0) 20 7620 1911
Website: www.msif.org/
The Multiple Sclerosis International Federation (MSIF) was established in 1967 as an international body linking the activities of National MS Societies around the world.

Further Reading

Coping with Multiple Sclerosis, by C. Benz;
Ebury Press, 1999

Multiple Sclerosis: A Personal Exploration,
by A. Burnfield; Souvenir Press, reprinted 2001

Multiple Sclerosis: A positive approach to living with MS, by C. McLaughlin (Editorial Consultant: A. Burnfield); Bloomsbury, 1997

Booklets and pamphlets

Don't Lose Your Balance
MS Society of Canada
Collection of stories from teenagers who have a parent with MS

Has your Mum or Dad got MS?
MS Society of Queensland, Australia

Keep S'myelin
NMSS of USA
Award-winning children's newsletter

My Dad's Got MS by G. Hetherington and
C. Young; MS Trust, UK, 2001
Booklet for children

Teen Inside MS
NMSS of USA
Colour mini-magazine written by and for teenagers living in a household where someone has MS

Disclaimer
All the Internet addresses (URLs) given in this book were valid at the time of going to press. However, due to the dynamic nature of the Internet, some addresses may have changed, or sites may have changed or ceased to exist since publication. While the author and Publisher regret any inconvenience this may cause readers, no responsibility for any such changes can be accepted by either the author or the Publisher.

Glossary

auto-immune response
when the immune system attacks the body's own tissues

benign MS
people with benign MS are not too badly affected

beta interferon
a drug used to lessen the effect of MS

bipolar disorder
mental illness in which severe depression alternates with periods of extreme excitement

catheter
tube inserted into the bladder to remove urine

central nervous system
brain and spinal cord

cerebrospinal fluid (CSF)
fluid surrounding the brain and spinal cord

clinical depression
a psychiatric illness in which a person becomes severely depressed and loses hope

clinical psychologist
a professional trained to help a person with concentration and behavior difficulties

corticosteroids
medication that dampens down inflammation

Creutzfeld-Jacob Disease (CJD)
an infective disease of the brain, known as 'mad cow' disease when it affects cattle

Epstein-Barr Virus (EBV)
a common virus that may cause a sore throat and tiredness for several weeks (glandular fever)

functional electrical stimulation (FES)
a process which uses special equipment to stimulate paralyzed muscles

gene
genes are found in our body cells and are passed on to us from our parents. They contain information that is the blueprint for everything about us, from eye colour to height.

glatiramer acetate
disease-modifying medication used to lessen the effect of MS

hallucinations
seeing things that are not there

heriditary
directly passed on from a parent to a child

Human Herpes Virus 6 (HHV-6)
a common virus that causes a rash called roseola in children

immune system
a system within the body that protects it against infection

immunology
the study of the immune system

incontinence
loss of control of the bladder

inflammation
swelling, in response to damage or infection

intermittent self-catheterization (ISC)
emptying the bladder by inserting a sterile tube when normal bladder control is unreliable

lesion
area of damage, for example a scar

lumbar puncture (spinal tap)
extracting a sample of the fluid surrounding the spinal cord

magnetic resonance image (MRI) scan
a special type of scan. An MRI scanner works using magnetic fields to produce an image.

myelin
a fatty substance protecting and surrounding the nerve fibres

neuralgia
intense nerve pain that comes and goes

neurological
to do with disorders of the nervous system

neurology
the study of nervous system disorders

Novantrone
a medication used to lessen the immune response and so modify the MS disease

occupational therapist
an expert in helping disabled people with the problems of everyday living

optic nerve
the nerve from the eye to the brain

pharmaceutical
to do with the production of medications

physiotherapist
an expert who helps people with physical disabilities to restore or improve movement

placebo
a substance with no medical action

plasma
the liquid part of blood

polyunsaturated fat
a food oil often found in fish. It helps nerves grow and work properly.

pressure sore
damage to skin that occurs when a person lies or sits in one position for too long

primary progressive MS
gradually worsening MS without remissions

psychiatric
to do with mental illness

rehabilitation
helping people to get back to normal life

relapse
sudden worsening of symptoms

relapsing/remitting MS (RRMS)
symptoms occurring from time to time, which then improve for a while, before returning

remission
recovery from MS symptoms after a relapse or attack

sclerosis
area of scarring, hardening of tissue

secondary progressive MS (SPMS)
gradual worsening of MS after a period of relapses and remissions

spasms
sudden, uncontrolled contraction of muscles

susceptibilty
tendency

tremor
uncontrolled shaking

urinary
to do with the bladder, the kidneys and the passing of urine

virology
the study of viruses

white blood cell
a cell that fights infection

Index

Titles in the *Need to Know* series include:

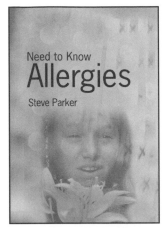

Need to Know
Allergies
Steve Parker

Hardback   0 431 09760 7

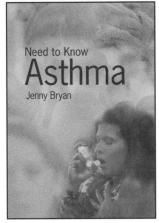

Need to Know
Asthma
Jenny Bryan

Hardback   0 431 09761 5

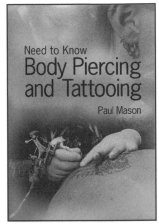

Need to Know
Body Piercing and Tattooing
Paul Mason

Hardback   0 431 09818 2

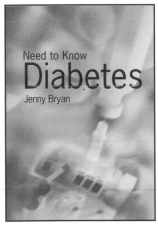

Need to Know
Diabetes
Jenny Bryan

Hardback   0 431 09762 3

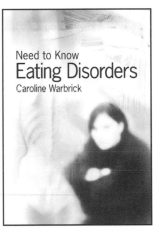

Need to Know
Eating Disorders
Caroline Warbrick

Hardback   0 431 09799 2

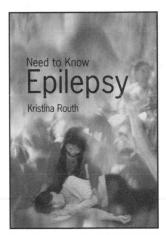

Need to Know
Epilepsy
Kristina Routh

Hardback   0 431 09763·1

Need to Know
Multiple Sclerosis
Alexander Burnfield

Hardback   0 431 09764 X

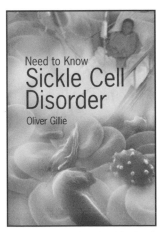

Need to Know
Sickle Cell Disorder
Oliver Gillie

Hardback   0 431 09765 8

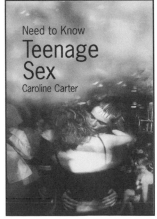

Need to Know
Teenage Sex
Caroline Carter

Hardback   0 431 09821 2

Find out about the other titles in this series on our website www.heinemann.co.uk/library